STORMS NEVER LAST

By
Laura Pouttu

To Shirley

Best wishes
Laura Pouttu

TEACH Services, Inc.
Brushton, New York

2008 09 10 11 12 13 14 · 5 4 3 2 1

Copyright © 2008 TEACH Services, Inc.
ISBN-13: 978-1-57258-545-4
ISBN-10: 1-57258-545-5
Library of Congress Control Number: 2008906163

Published by

TEACH Services, Inc.
www.TEACHServices.com

CHAPTER 1

The early 1950s, Buffalo, New York. A young high-school-aged couple from poor, broken homes need each other. They trust and hope for each other and want a better life. They marry and rent a cold-water flat in Buffalo NY, and start a life together.

Their names are Ron and Donna. Two years pass, and they are blessed with their first child, Tonya. She's a quiet, smart little girl, with brown wavy hair. Every two years they are again blessed with a child: Ron Jr., a rough-and-tumble little boy, followed by Jennifer, a pretty little princess. Times are hard, but their love seems to carry them through.

Donna's mom and step dad decide to move to a warmer climate. They decide to move to Arizona, and Donna and Ron soon follow. There they have two more children: Veronica, a delicate, quiet little girl, followed by me, Lori, a busy, inquisitive little girl. For parents of five children, times are very hard. My mother stays at home with us children while my daddy tries to make a living to support us all.

My dad has a hard time finding work in Arizona. He's doing his best to make the best of what he has, but with no jobs available, my parents decide to move to California. We leave Arizona, and my father quickly finds a full time job.

Daddy works long hours to feed the family. He often comes home tired and with little patience. The older children seem to sense this and scurry off to their room to play. I often get into trouble for talking too much and racing from one place to the next. I have too many questions and too much energy for a tired working man.

Even though my daddy works long hours, he never has enough money to care for a large family.

My parents often allow family members and friends to live with us; the rent that they pay helps my parents make ends meet. This of course excites me even more, and I roam from one family to the next, talking. I also listen carefully to what is being said so that I can share the information with others. This, too, gets me into a great deal of trouble. I'm the black sheep.

CHAPTER 2

When I'm two years old, I am outside playing while everybody is busy working. I run too fast and too far into the street. I'm hit by a car. I fly in the air and land in the next-door neighbor's yard, on the left side of my body. I'm rushed to the hospital, where I'm told I have only bruises—and medical bills.

Months later I spike a fever of 106 degrees, going into convulsions and I return to the hospital. This adds to my daddy's frustration. As bills keep coming in, the other four children stay healthy.

When I'm three years old, my Uncle Jay and Aunt Sharon come to stay until they are able to get an apartment; they stay in Tonya's room. I'm beside myself with excitement. New people to talk to and follow around! On their first night, Uncle Jay and Aunt Sharon go to bed. Five minutes later the door opens, and there I stand, a little blond-haired child ready to climb into their bed and talk some more. My daddy hears my voice, and with a loud yell, "Laura!" he removes me from the room. Sadly I go off to my own bed, where the other children are fast asleep and there is nobody to talk to.

This is when I start to act strangely. I have terrible fears. I constantly feel that someone is going to get me. The terror lasts for only short periods, but leaves me feeling scared. I feel safer when I can stay close to my mother.

Once again my mother is pregnant. She gives birth to a baby boy. Mom is really happy to welcome another boy into the family but, sadly, the baby dies shortly after birth.

CHAPTER 3

I'm now four to five years old. I continue to have these panic attacks. They are lasting longer. I rub my hands together and lick my lips as my mouth becomes very hot. I continue to have that feeling like someone is going to get me. I tell my mother how I feel and she tells me, "Nobody is going to hurt you. Stop acting up."

Yearly visits back to Arizona to visit my mother's family are not fun for me. I follow family members around, asking questions. They become annoyed with me, and my daddy yells at me to go watch TV, but I don't like TV. It never seems to interest me. This is where my love of birds begins—my grandmother has a talking parrot.

The strange feelings continue to occur, now up to three or four times a week. Of course my parents think this is little Lori's way of getting attention. I try hard to listen to my mother. I go outside to go skating and play with the other children. One day I'm skating, having the panic attacks. My mouth is hot. I have the fear that someone is coming to get me. Next thing, I'm picking myself up with a bloody mouth. I have run into a pole, chipping my front tooth. I don't know how this happened; only that I had a funny feeling just before it did.

My mother becomes pregnant again, giving birth to a pretty little girl named Patricia. Now, in the proud family of six children, life is even harder. But my mother loves us all with her heart and soul.

I'm just six when I overhear a discussion by my parents and neighbors. They speak of a neighbor lady who always wears the same clothes and appears dirty. The next morning I go into my mother's closet to get a pretty dress and some of my mom's jewelry. I take it to the neighbor, so that they will not talk about her any more. The plan backfires. The lady returns the items to my mother, explaining that I have given them to her. That night my daddy comes home from work. My mother tells him what I have done. My daddy sits me down by the table, asking me, "Where did you get this dress?" I answer, very excitedly, "In mommy's closet." My daddy hits me across my face and head very hard for my effort to help a neighbor. I'm asked, "Where did you get the earrings?" I don't want to be hit again. I answer, "I don't know." That causes even more problems. He starts hitting me with the belt. I'm now put on restriction for a month. This makes no sense to a child six years old; I thought I had done something good.

This is where music comes into my life. I play my mother's albums over and over, enjoying the music singing into my ears.

CHAPTER 4

I'm now seven. My parents purchase their first home. It is a large home. My daddy's brother, Frank, returns from the military and stays with the family until he can get settled down. This is when the sexual abuse starts. I do not know what to do. I'm a little girl; he is an adult who I'm told to mind. Frank tells me he will tell my daddy if I do not listen, and I will be hit with the belt again. Knowing what the belt feels like, I keep this a secret for quite some time.

One evening my sister and I talk. I find out that my sister is also being abused. We talk about telling, but I'm afraid because I think I will be punished. I don't want to be hit again. Our mother overhears the conversation and goes to my dad. My daddy has a real hard time with this; he does not want to believe that his brother is hurting us girls. He drills me with questions, making me feel like it's all my fault or it didn't really happen. He finally believes me and disowns his brother.

Again I feel like I'm a disappointment to my daddy. In my little head I feel I have again caused trouble. The only time I seem calm and at peace is when I can sit in my room and listen to music. I escape into another world when the music plays. I'm sent to my room often, and my love of music grows. My room is a safe place where nobody is angry with me. I sing along and escape to the place the song speaks of. I'm a little girl in need of a daddy's love and praise.

CHAPTER 5

I meet a man named Fred who lives just up the street. He is kind to me. He never yells. He teaches me how to use a drill and sander, and how to make money to buy the things I want. I finally have a father figure. I run around collecting cans to buy clothes, toys and other things I want. I'm learning how to make things with my hands. Finally, I have a way to burn off some of my energy. I have a dream that some day I will own two houses—one to live in, and one to open a daycare center. My center will be a place where all children will feel safe and loved.

I keep myself busy going up the street to Fred's house, learning how to make things and how to make money.

Things seem quiet for a year; the quiet ends in a big way. On Christmas day, I'm having the panic attacks, one after another, and I am brought to the hospital. I'm given a shot of valium and referred to a neurologist. After a year of being yelled at and slapped, they learn I *actually do* have a medical problem.

The attacks continue and my daddy continues to yell, stating that I can stop the attacks if I want to. This, of course, is not true. I'm now starting to act really strange. I'm very quiet and just look off into space. This, too, annoys my daddy; he feels I have found a new way to get attention. This continues for a year before I'm taken to the doctor, only to have the doctor say, "She's doing it for attention." My daddy is very angry and starts slapping me on the head, saying, "You get that look off your face." as I go into my far-away stare. Again I escape to Fred's house. I always wished *he* could be my dad. He has lots of patience with me. He gives me my first radio, and again I escape into music. Fred gives me a job watering his lawn and allows me to just sit and listen to my music. My mommy loves me and tries hard to keep me out of my daddy's way. She knows I love music and buys me a stereo so I can make my own tapes from off the radio. This serves two purposes: it keeps me busy and in my room.

CHAPTER 6

The attacks become uncontrollable. My daddy and mommy decide I need medical attention. I'm taken to UCLA, where I'm put on one medication after another. But it is to no avail. The only thing it does is cause my school work to go downhill. Again my dad is very angry. Now I'm lazy, too. My sisters manage to earn A's and B's. I, on the other hand, am lucky to get a C or a D.

I'm at UCLA. The neurologist is explaining that those funny feelings are called auras, and that they are warnings that a seizure is about to occur. This gives me time to sit down in a safe area. I learn that seizures happen when there is a sudden burst of electrical discharge of brain cells — an electrical brain storm. My auras cause a funny taste in my mouth; my tongue gets hot, I lick my lips and have to rub my hands, and don't want anybody close to me except my mommy.

I'm excited. Summer vacation is coming and we are going to visit our grandmother. This is going to be great.

It isn't. My grandmother sees me as cursed by the devil and will have nothing to do with me. My Grandma invites Jennifer and Veronica to stay for a month, but not me. Again I feel like a black sheep. The older girls are quiet and entertain themselves. I, on the other hand, follow grandma around asking questions. Sadly, I climb back into the car for the long trip home without my sisters, and feel so low. I don't know how to make people like me.

Once back home I work even harder to make money. It seems like this is the only thing that gets me any praise. Fred encourages me to put half of my money in the bank and keep half for myself, and I do. I hit the three-hundred-dollar mark. I'm so proud. Fred continues to teach me how to make money. Finally, something I'm good at.

Again the new medication is having a bad effect on me. I'm tired and sick to my stomach most of the time. I lie in bed and listen to the radio. I'm the fifth caller in a radio station contest, and win the album of my choice. I play "You and Me" over and over, driving everyone in the house crazy.

My daddy has a heart attack which limits his ability to do some of the work around the house. I see my mommy looking out the kitchen window at our yard. The skills I have learned are needed. I go into my daddy's garage, take the mower out, and mow the lawn. I ask Fred if he could help me edge the sidewalk. Fred meets my mom and dad while he edges the sidewalk area. I water and pick fruit from the trees, making sure everything looks great. Perhaps my dad will finally realize that I am of some value. My mom is shocked at how well I handle all the yard work. I'm only nine and can keep the yard perfect. Wow! Praise from mom is great.

I really love my mother and I show her by buying her flowers when I have extra money. My mother is my protector on most occasions. My mother doesn't yell or slap me like my dad does.

CHAPTER 7

I continue to learn new jobs when my medication doesn't keep me down. I become the neighborhood kid whom everyone can use. I run errands for people, drop off dry-cleaning, and pick the clothes up and return them. I always have a big smile for people as I run errands to make money.

After my dad had his heart attack, money is even tighter. I do not realize how tight until I go to the bank to put money in, only to discover that my money has been taken out. I'm so angry. I run to Fred's house to show him. He gives me a bicentennial bank and tells me to keep my money in it so that nobody else can take it. My heart is broken, as I have worked so hard and have been so proud of myself for earning the money. My anger carries home. I want to know, "Why have you taken my money?" I'm told they had hoped to put it back before I noticed it gone. They had to pay bills. I'm too young to understand . . .

I'm just entering the fifth grade. I'm signed up for the glee club. I really love music but I can't carry a tune. My teacher tells me to sing in a lower voice, so I just start to lip sing so I can stay in the glee club. I love this class. Piano lessons are offered after school. I want to take piano lessons. I ask my mother, "Can I stay after school?" I explain that she will have to pick me up or I could wait for the 5:00 bus. My mother says, "No, you just come right home on the regular bus." I don't understand why my sisters can stay after school for activities, but I always have to come home.

I'm our class's number-one fundraiser—I can outsell anyone.

I'm in the sixth grade. I'm working very hard to get better grades, to be like my sisters. I get all A's on my report card; I'm so excited to let my dad see how well I have done. My dad comes home from work as the family sits down to dinner. When dinner is over, my dad goes into the living room. I go up to him, showing him my report card. He looks it over, seeing all A's. He tosses it back on the table. He says, "That's what I want to see." Then he turns and walks away. I'm hurt. I tell myself, "I guess D's are just as good as A's."

Again I will cost my dad money. When I'm in the eighth grade, I'm given a note stating that I need glasses. Of course my daddy sees this as another "Lori" problem. My older siblings are now in high school and involved in band and other activities that cost money. My dad and mom join the booster club, telling me to give the money from my cans to the high-school band booster. I'm angry. I don't feel it is fair, but I do what my daddy has told me to do.

My parents are starting a soap business, selling soaps and other things to try to get rich fast. My daddy really believes in this business and he takes out a loan to stock up on everything. One bedroom becomes an office; there goes my own bedroom. My parents put all of their money into the business, even going to a car dealer and leasing a Lincoln Continental. My daddy works hard and sets out to get everybody he knows to join under him, family and friends. I can't see paying that much money for soap. Again I'm too young to understand.

CHAPTER 8

I'm fourteen. I start high school, but the seizures are taking control of my life. Each new medication only works for a short time and has many side effects. I'm working hard to just make D's.

Time moves on. I'm now in the tenth grade. I'm signed up for driver education, only to find out that people with seizures are not allowed to drive. This is another blow to an already heartbroken young girl.

I have signed up for physical education and am removed from that, too, as I can have a seizure and get hurt. Two things I want and need are not going to happen. One class that I'm able to keep is typing. This comforts me as I enjoy at least one good elective class.

The three older siblings are starting to move out of the house and I finally get my own room. What a joy! I can listen to my music as much as I want. The joy is short-lived as my mom and dad again take in a family member and give them my room.

In my junior year, my parents decide to sell their house to move out of the area. This is traumatic for me. I now have to go to a new school where the kids and teachers do not know about my seizures. I take required classes and one class off campus. I have to walk three blocks to take a data processing class. I'm walking back to school. I have a seizure and drop all of my papers. The wind catches them and they blow all over. I finally come out of it. I'm very tired and need to rest. I'm grateful that I did not run into the street or do something worse.

The family business is starting to go downhill and my mother is having a hard time keeping up with the bills. Leasing a car costs a lot of money, but they have to keep it until the lease is up. Things are becoming even tougher when my parents begin renting. I can't understand why someone would go from one level down to a lower one. It's an education for me to learn that bills come before play.

CHAPTER 9

It's my senior year. I'm taking a class on the psychology of family living. I really love this class and choose adoption for my area of study. A girl named Debbie and I work on a project together. Debbie is able to set up a guest speaker on the topic. When the speaker begins her presentation, I feel a seizure coming on. The signs are always the same. My mouth is hot and I have that scared feeling, like someone is going to get me. I hurry to leave the room to have the seizure in the hallway. My teacher is wonderful. She stays by my side until I feel better.

The class is a success; I receive a high grade. I manage to graduate mid-term in February 1982 by working very hard. I'm in a hurry to get out of school, as people look at me funny when I have a seizure. I don't know anybody in our new home town. I can't work or drive.

I call Fred to tell him I finished high school. I'm still having uncontrolled seizures, and I can't have a normal life with seizures. Fred is starting to have serious medical problems. He sells his truck and can't work anymore. I tell him that if I could drive I would do his work. He says, "You don't want to get into the trucking business." I tell him I love him very much and I hang up the phone.

Things are not going well at the house. My daddy tells me that I need to get a job and start paying rent or get out. I apply for state aid and I'm provided a small check to help meet my needs. But I don't want state aid. I want a job like my older siblings. The fear of having uncontrolled seizures keeps me from getting one.

I'm 18 years old and make a major decision—to have my tubes tied. Having lived with seizures and enduring much abuse, I know I don't want to bring any children into the world to suffer like I have. I go to a place to watch a video that goes over steps that may be important if you're not sure about the procedure. I can't see bringing children into the world having to live with my seizures. I go to have my tubes cut and tied. I believe that there are many children in this world who need love. I can give love; they don't have to be mine.

CHAPTER 10

I start to take control of my own destiny. I contact my neurologist and tell him that I can't live with the uncontrolled seizures any more, and that I need some real help. The medications are not doing anything for me. The neurologist signs me up for more study programs to see if brain surgery can be done. He sets me up for Phase I of an experimental program at UCLA.

My mother's standing by my side, telling me to never give up. I'm hooked up to the EEG electrodes. I'm having no pain. The system is on my head, wrapped up for testing 24 hours a day for two weeks.

I have another test, called a Pneumoencephalogram; it's a very painful test. They strap me to a chair as if I'm going to be electrocuted, ready to die. Liquid is pulled out of my spine and air is injected into my brain. The pain is excruciating. It's a test I would never wish on anybody.

When the test is complete, I have to lie on my back for many hours, making it hard for me to use the bathroom. I have to use the bathroom and call for a nurse. She says that I have to use the bedpan. How do I use the bedpan lying flat on my back? I'm in a lot of pain, asking the nurses to use a catheter. I can't urinate lying down. I ask the nurses to let me sit up to urinate. They say I have to stay flat on my back. I again say that I can't urinate lying on my back. I'm ready to jump off the bed to use the toilet. The nurse says that she has a catheter on order. I say, "You should have had it on hand." The nurse finally uses a catheter. The pain makes me not want to drink or eat anything until I know I can move around.

These tests last a full two weeks. They set up an appointment for me to speak to a psychiatrist to discuss my feelings about everything I have been through. I just want my seizures to stop.

Here we are starting a new day hoping everything comes out great. A psychiatrist takes me into a room that has a very large window. It's only me and this man in the room. He starts asking me questions. I have no idea who he is. I have no interest in talking. I don't feel that I should see a psychiatrist. I'm not in for being crazy. It's a waste of time and money in my view. By this time, after years of neurologists claiming that I have seizures for attention, I trust no doctors. He says, "Nobody is in this room. You can talk about anything." He brings up hobbies, friends, games. Nothing works. I tell him, "I have nothing to talk about. All I want is for the seizures to stop so I can be like normal people." He asks, "Are you being abused?" Again I say nothing. I ask, "Can I go back to my room?" All I get with this man is wasted money, and his verdict that I'm faking seizures. He's not able to get any information out of me. He writes that I've been abused.

The first week I have no seizures, but during the second week the seizures are almost back-to-back. The doctor jokes, "Okay Lori, you can stop now." I look at him and say "If only I could." My mother is proud of me for taking the steps to put an end to this misery.

My dad comes home from work very upset one day and asks if he can wear my tee shirt that reads, "If you're looking for a job you can have mine." I give it to him. He wears it to work the next day. My daddy has been working at the same job for many years, a position that he has put in for is given to a woman with less experience and seniority. My daddy quits his job with no way to pay bills.

Mom gives the thirty-day moving notice and we move into Jennifer's home. Her home isn't very big. In time we move into a two-bedroom apartment.

Unknown to me, my mother is very sick. She seems tired all of the time and her back hurts. She goes to a chiropractor for an adjustment, but has even more pain. My dad feels the financial need again, and tells me I will have to pay more rent or get out. I argue with him, saying, "Can't you see mom is in a great deal of pain? She doesn't need a chiropractor. She needs a real doctor." Angry and frustrated he screams back that the chiropractor is helping and to mind my own business. I tell my dad, "When my mother is lying in the casket dead, I will tell you she isn't dead; that she needs a chiropractor."

I storm out of the house very angry and move into a laundromat for shelter. The owner lets me open and close it. I do what is needed. I meet many people, including a man name Charlie, and we become good friends. Charlie tells me that he once had a very bad sinus infection that blocked his head so badly that he was in a coma for a month. It affected his memory and he now has to take seizure medication. He doesn't have seizures as long as he takes it. He understands my challenges due to living with seizures. Charlie does his laundry at the same time that my mother and I do ours. My mother really likes Charlie. They always talk.

My mom continues to get worse. She becomes weaker as time goes by. The phone rings. It's some people calling to let me know that Fred, my friend who was like a *real* father, was found dead. Life for me has hit an all-time low. He was such a special person. I thank the people who called.

My dad found another job; I sneak over to see my mother when he is at work. I tell her, "If I could drive, you wouldn't be in this bed, dying." I love my mother. I ask her, "If God takes you away, will you ask him to take away these uncontrolled seizures?" My mother smiles, saying, "Yes." I hug my mother and leave.

CHAPTER 11

My mother dies on December 8, 1985. Two days later a phone call comes my way. It's my neurologist, telling me my name just came up to have Phase II. I start crying; the doctor has no idea I just lost my mother. He asks, "Is there a problem?" I answer, "I just lost my mother two days ago." The neurologist says, "We can set yours back." I say no very firmly. "I can see the light—my mother spoke to God and now the time is here." The doctor replies, "I want you in by December 18." I say, "I will make sure that I will be there."

I call my sisters and brother to let them know I will undergo more testing. My dad starts crying and says, "No Lori, I can't lose another family member." I assure him that my mother is with God and is lighting the path for me. I explain that if he were unable to drive or go to work, and had to live on the streets, he too would go through with the next phase. At this point in my life, my sister Jennifer is also trying to help me be independent by teaching me the bus routes. This might have worked if I were able to control the seizures.

Dad says, "I will not be with you after just losing my wife." I understand. My brother again picks me up and takes me to UCLA. I'm checked into the hospital and meet with the doctor. He takes the time to go over the effects of the testing. I ask, "Is this test like the Pneumoencephalogram?" The doctor smiles and says, "No." I'm checked into my room to get ready for more testing. The following day they shaved my hair off my head. My hair is gone. It's a feeling I will never forget. Then the nails are drilled into my head and hooked up with the electrodes that go deeper into my skull.

Phase II begins on December 19, 1985. During Phase II most people have headaches. Nurses ask me, "Do you have any pain?" I answer, "No." This is like Phase I, except the electrodes go deeper into the skull to find more information. I'm now being set up for the Wada test, which puts one side of the brain to sleep at a time. It finds information on how my brain is set up. I'm finding this test very interesting.

Christmas day arrives and the family comes to see me. Tonya says, "Dad can't take hospitals." I say, "It's no problem," knowing that my mother is still by my side. Time goes by. My daddy comes to see me. I say, "I have no pain. I just hope this test will show doctors that I can have the major brain surgery in order to live my life."

I have the aura. A seizure is about to occur. I push the button and yell, "Time!" The nurses run into my room, one on each side of me, as another one calls out my actions. My lips smack, my hands rub, and my body shakes. The nurses ask me questions: "What is your name?" I go into the seizure. I'm unconscious. I'm hoping everything will be caught on the test that is needed to make the seizures stop. I asked question after question, making sure I learn like the doctors. It's done on January 19, 1986.

CHAPTER 12

I return to the Laundromat. People see me without any hair. I say, "I want to try punk rock, it's in style." I've always been a strong, positive person. I've never let anything get me down. The phone rings. It's my neurologist, calling to let me know he is ready to set me up for major brain surgery. Phase III will take place. On April 9, 1986, I'm to be at UCLA. The surgery will take place the following day. I say, "That's my sister's anniversary. It must be lucky." I'm so excited.

I call my brother and ask, "Can you please take me to the hospital on April ninth?" I tell my daddy I'm having Phase III. My daddy is more relaxed and tells me to make my own decision about what I want for my future. He will be at the hospital for the surgery.

Ron Jr. picks me up; I'm ready for Phase III. I check into UCLA. Again they shave my head to remove all of the hair that has grown back. They set everything up for the major brain surgery. I'm told that this surgery will affect my memory. It can also affect my vision and speech. I say, "Seizures already do that. It won't be much different." I'm at the point where I have nothing to lose. On the following day I'm taken into the operating room. They set me all up as I smile at my dad. I say, "My mother is still by my side." They put the mask on my face and tell me to take a deep breath. I go to sleep; and the brain surgery takes place.

I regain consciousness in the recovery room, and find my daddy sitting by my bed, reading a book. I smile and tell him, "I told you not to worry; God isn't ready for me yet." Unlike with the last surgery, I'm in a great deal of pain. The neurologist warns me that my memory is not intact. I can remember some, but not much. I will remain in the hospital for eight days. Eight days is a long time for me. I'm not a person to just sit around.

Many doctors come into the room at once to see how I'm doing. They start asking questions. The doctor points to a clock and asks me, "Can you tell me what this is?" I have no idea how to say *clock*. All I can do is describe it. "It's something that people put on the wall." I point to the doctor's watch and say, "It's the same thing." I can't say *clock*. It makes me very aggravated. I know what it is and I can't say it.

It is really hard to rest at the hospital. Just as I get to sleep, the nurses come to take my blood pressure, or do some procedure that wakes me up. I make sure that I get out of bed to walk around. Trying to remember things isn't easy. The neurosurgeon comes into the room. I ask, "Can't I go home?" He smiles and says, "Not just yet, it takes about eight days." I say, "Eight days in a hospital?" He says, "Just rest." I say, "I have a lot to get done. I don't want to stay brainless." He tells me that he doesn't want me to get my hopes up too high. This isn't a 100% surgery. I smile and say, "You did your part. Now it's up to me to do my part of the job." He laughs and tells me to rest. I have plenty of time.

Eight days later my brother comes to pick me up. The doctors explain that I have a 50/50 chance of having additional seizures. I have such high hopes; I don't want to think about seizures. I want a life like my siblings. I tell the neurologist to give me twenty years to relearn, to drive, to work and to build a future in life. The doctor tells me to rest.

My brother arrives in his Corvette, which of course is not a comfortable ride for someone who has just had brain surgery. He drops me off at daddy's house. My head is in a lot of pain; it pounds. I go to sleep until my daddy wakes me up. The next day I turn on the T.V, something I don't usually do, and hear a girl sing a song called "He's still working on me." It gives me a feeling that this is a message sent my way from my mother. Tonya stops by to see me. I'm rubbing my stomach really hard. Tonya asks me if my stomach is hurting. I answer, "No." My head hurts really bad.

CHAPTER 13

For someone who has just had brain surgery, the laundromat is not a place to live. I go to live with my sister Tonya. Tonya has two children, and I can help care for the children in exchange for room and board. I love the children and enjoy my time with them. I play ball and board games. I walk the older child to the school-bus stop and go home and play with the little one. The children love to rub my bald head.

It's time to take my nephew to the bus stop. He says, "You can drop me off at the corner." He doesn't want other children to see my bald head. I can understand. I drop him off at the corner. He runs the rest of the way to the bus stop. I stand at the corner until the bus comes, to make sure he is off to school.

It's time to pick the children up from the bus stop. I make sure I stay at the corner until he runs up to me. He comes back, saying that his friends really like my bald head. They all want to feel it. I let the children feel my head. The children want me to come to the bus stop.

The little one starts kindergarten, so I'm taking both children to the bus stop to send them to school. The day comes when it's time for the children to come home from school on the bus. The bus is here to drop them off. The older one steps off the bus, but the little one doesn't. He comes running off the bus crying, "I left my brother at school."

I can't drive. I tell him to calm down. I say, "Let's go on bicycles to find him." I call the school to ask if they can look to see if the child is out front. I want them to make sure he stays there until I pick him up. We take off on the bikes. We arrive at the school, and there he is standing in front of the school, crying. I give him a hug, and tell him it's okay. We take off and we stop at the ice cream store. I give them each an ice cream.

I'm ready to have my own room. I move in with my brother Ron Jr. We agree to split the rent and utilities. I use the disability check to cover my share. I start college and apply for a disability-student program so I can continue my education and have purpose in life. I apply for a bus pass so that I can get where I need to be without being dependent on others. I'm making some great strides in becoming what I consider normal.

I enjoy knitting and making gifts for people. I'm finding the person I can be. I find the people in the world to be kind and friendly. The bus drivers always greet me with a smile, and all of the regulars are glad to see me. I come across some drivers who look at me as a person who can probably drive. They don't think that I need a disability bus pass and ask to see my ID. I smile and say, "I wish people like you worked at the DMV." I let them see my ID so that they know it's good. What a different world than the one I had grown up in! Even though my hair is just coming back in and I look like a punk rocker, I'm being accepted.

CHAPTER 14

Going to college is challenging, as concentrating is very difficult. The memory part of my brain has to be retrained. It's time to work on my dream: having two houses, one for children and the other for me to live in. My focus at college is child-development classes.

One of the speakers really makes me angry. She says that victims of abuse go on to abuse others. I know that I would never hurt a child like I was hurt. I speak out at this lady, saying, "It isn't true—look at all the people who have been abused who don't hurt any children. You're giving sick people excuses." The speaker shares that she will have to see both sides, and thanks me for speaking out.

Classes are a challenge for me. I have to tape everything and replay it many times to get the concept of what is being taught. Relearning makes life hard. It's a lot of work. Also, I am unable to drive. Since I have to be at places on time and I take buses that just miss each other, I have to sit for an hour here and there. My Walkman sure does its part, singing into my ears. It helps keep me stronger, wanting to get better faster, to work harder.

Things are not going well with my brother. He starts to take advantage of me by eating my food and not coming up with his share of the bills. I try to put it aside, knowing how my brother took me to the doctor appointments.

Then my brother lets a friend of his stop by. He brings a drug called cocaine. He tells me that if I want to get rid of my pain, all I have to do is snort a line of this stuff. He rolls up a dollar bill and sniffs the white powder. This really opens my eyes; I now know that they do drugs and that money can be left with drug residue on it.

I spend as much time out of the apartment as I can with a friend, Alice, who lives next door. Things become even worse when my brother allows his girlfriend to move in. Now I'm paying most of the bills for three people and don't feel at home. I have to lock my bedroom door and hide my things there to keep them safe. I approach the landlord and ask if I can just get a one-bedroom for myself. He agrees. My life on my own begins. Wow, what an awesome feeling! My house, my food, my furniture . . . I'm becoming a real person.

It's hard at first. Gas and electric deposits are more than I have. I have a bed in a one-bedroom apartment, without utilities. I know people from the church, and one kind person contacts the church to help me get the utilities turned on, and to get some furniture. The lady from the church says she has a cheap couch for sale, and I call to arrange to go and see it. The husband answers, saying that the lady has just stepped out, but that he can come pick me up to show me the couch.

He knows I cannot drive. He comes and picks me up to see the couch. I'm not afraid. I think they are both God-fearing people. I'm wrong. When the man takes me to the house to see the couch he attempts to sexually assault me. He grabs me around the neck to lay me down. I fight him off. It takes me back to the time when I was a child and my uncle had done the same thing. My faith in people is again tested. I fight him off and run out of the house. I can't drive, and I have no money to call someone to come get me. I'm five miles from my home. It's a moment I will never forget. I will not return to that church.

A year later, I have paid my bills on time. The deposits are returned. I take the money back to church, thanking them. I continue my friendship with Alice, my brother's neighbor. I help Alice with her grandchildren, and even travel to Mexico with them. I purchase parrot cages to start raising birds. I start training my parrots to talk and sing. I really enjoy it. The parrots love the attention. Birds are a safety item for me. They can't hurt me and just want to be loved and cared for. Alice and I become closer. Alice starts to drive me to my doctor appointments, gets food, and does any errands. In exchange, I clean her house and look after her grandchildren.

CHAPTER 15

I have my own place with my birds. Charlie and I are becoming closer. He treats me better than my family has treated me. Charlie and I decide to rent a place together, and we become a couple. We share a two-bedroom and split all costs. This makes financial life for me easier.

It's time to go see my neurologist. I go for my appointment. I share everything I have been working on after my brain surgery. My neurologist is leaving UCLA and asks me, "Who do you want to go under?" Dr. Sam has been with me. I say, "I want Dr. Sam." He wishes me the best of luck as he leaves UCLA. I have been under Dr. Sam's care off and on, and he knows my history.

I go see Dr. Sam. He tells me, "I'm not sure if I can continue medical treatment. I'm booked up with many patients." I say, "I won't be a rough patient. I will only need medications refilled if needed, and I'll only need brain tests updated if something comes up. It's now up to me to finish off my part after phase III." He says, "It should be good." I leave his office telling myself it's a sign that I don't need medication. I finish up the medications, knowing I don't need seizure medication any more.

CHAPTER 16

A phone call comes my way. It's my cousin from Oklahoma. She wants me to come to Florida on vacation with her and her family. I have never had a vacation; my life has consisted of doctors and hospitals. Charlie tells me to go and enjoy life. I purchase a plane ticket and fly off to Oklahoma. I'm picked up at the airport by my cousin Gloria and her children.

It's all farmland. My dream of two homes in the country comes back to me even stronger. Gloria shows me everything, even where to go if a tornado hits. The second morning a wild donkey walks up to the fence. After life in a big city this is an unreal experience. Gloria tells me to be careful of it. It is so pretty and the setting is just amazing. I go to the fence and start to hand feed the animal.

Country living is so different. Gloria shows me how to use a ringer washer. I have no idea these things still exist. We have to drain the tub and use the ringer to get the water out. Then we have to hang the clothes to dry. The clothes are as stiff as a board when the process is complete.

The next day Gloria takes me to see a friend named Joey, who has a cow farm. He's a really nice guy who works very hard. Gloria decides to invite Joey to Florida with us. I think that's a real good idea, as Joey works very hard on his farm. I keep feeling like this is the type of life I'm meant to live. Country living is my thing.

We start off on our trip to Florida. Gloria, her husband and their three children, Joey and I are packed into their old Plymouth Fury. We sing songs and stop along the side of the road to see sights in Louisiana. We see ponds with alligators in them.

Soon the car breaks down and we have to stay in a motel. The three children are wired for sound; they have been cooped up in the car for long periods of time. Then my gift with children comes into play. I play with the children while the men sleep, so that they can be rested for the next phase of our trip.

We arrive safely in Florida. There are many things to see. We go to the beach and take boogie boards, surfing the waves. I'm taking in every precious moment of this trip. We go to see Cape Canaveral. The next day will be Disney World. We load up and head that way, only to be stopped by a bad thunderstorm.

Sadly, it's time to end the trip and head back to Oklahoma. We never made it to Disney World. My first real vacation has ended, but I've made happy memories that will carry though to my future life.

CHAPTER 17

My neurologist calls, sharing that he is leaving UCLA to join The Epilepsy and Brain Mapping Program. It's a new program for brain disorders. I say, "It's still right here, close to me. I will just follow you to this building." I continue to see Dr. Sam. I'm not ready to start over with a new neurologist. Neurologists have no idea what it takes to start with new doctors. Doctors always want you to start over new, but I want to move forward.

Through the years, people have given me their opinions on what I should study in college, or what I should do with my life. I don't want to be a computer person. I want to be a child-care provider. I'm told that being a babysitter isn't a job that pays. I tell the people that I want to own two houses, one for children and one to live in, to do what I love. I want to live next to the childcare place so I don't have to drive. I don't want to depend on a car. People just tell me I'm wasting time and money. I say, "You will see that someday my dream will be fulfilled."

Charlie and I purchase property in Idaho. There are two houses on the lot. My dream will come true. A call comes my way. It's my daddy, wanting everybody to meet at Tonya's house for a family meeting. He tells everybody he is dying of cancer and wants to get rid of everything in his house. He asks everybody what they want. He asks me, "Is there anything that you want?" I say, "I only want my mother's records." My dad says, "Those go to Tonya." I have no interest in anything else. They set up a name-drawing for things. My name comes up for the TV games. I have no interest in games. I give them to the nephews to enjoy. It sure makes their day. My daddy passes away in 1990.

CHAPTER 18

Charlie receives notice that his job is going to transfer him a hundred miles away. After much thought I decide that I'm not really close to anyone in my family, and that I might as well go with him. The big break from family and friends will give me a chance to start over, where nobody knows my history.

Charlie and I find an apartment in Oxnard, California, and we are quite excited about the move. We find an apartment and return home to pack our belongings. We return to get the new apartment, but we are given keys to an apartment other than the one we had chosen. Charlie has a good job just three miles from the house. The future looks bright. Our belongings fit perfectly. Even my birds fit. I love our new place. I take great pride in keeping it clean. I move the furniture and redecorate it on a regular basis. But regardless of how much I clean, our new apartment always has a funny smell. We are told it's been vacant for quite a while; "Just open the windows and let it air out." I do just that, yet the smell will not leave. Soon we both become sick with a hacking cough that we cannot shake.

I love my birds and purchase a bird magazine. To my amazement, I find that I can purchase toys for them. I find a company that makes parrot bikes. I know my parrot Ernie will enjoy a bike, so I order one. It arrives, and I start to train my birds. I always think that Ernie's a male parrot until I have him tested and learn that she's a female. I still call her Ernie. She likes to skateboard for French fries or a strawberry ice cream. Everybody loves her. I send the magazine a picture of Ernie riding her bike. I watch at the stores to see Ernie's picture make it. What an exciting moment.

I'm always thinking. I realize that the lady next door works for a movie company. I take Ernie to her house, to let her watch Ernie ride her bike and roller skate. I ask "Can I use the large window on your patio to tape the parrot riding her bike?" The neighbor's husband comes out to help as we tape Ernie riding. I tape all of the parts of the Song "Brand New Key" and make a video of the parrots. It comes out great. It gives everybody a great laugh.

It's been a busy day; I'm really tired and get myself ready for bed. I lie down and go to sleep and start to dream. I'm with a family at a cemetery in the office. The people have a couple of children. I say, "My parents are buried just over the hill. I will show the children while you take care of business." I take the children and we run over the hill to my mother's grave. We arrive and see everybody sitting in lounge chairs, visiting. I say, "Is that you, Mom?" She says, "Yes." I ask, "I thought you were dead?" She says, "We are dead honey, can't you see?" I say, "Dead people stay in a casket underground." My mother laughs and says, "See that hole where people put flowers?" I answer, "Yes." She says, "That's where we come out of each day. We all visit. Then at 5:00 p.m. we all get ready to go to sleep." I'm in shock at seeing my mother again. She's telling me never to worry about her. She is at rest and is in no pain. She says, "I'm always watching over you, making sure you're doing a great job." The children's parents call. I tell my mother, "We have to go." I give her a big hug and tell her, "I love you very much." She tells me, "Never give up. Hold strong no matter what comes your way." The children and I start running back to the parents as we wave good-bye to my mother. I wake up.

I cannot go back to sleep, thinking about my mother. I lie there, thinking about this dream, wondering what made me dream it. It makes me feel good to know that she is still looking over me. I take this dream as a message. She can't talk to me in person; she did it in a dream. I slowly fall back to sleep until the next day.

CHAPTER 19

I go to see my neurologist. He says, "You're doing great, and now you can get a driver's license." I head home to tell Charlie my good news. I ask him, "Can you please teach me how to drive?" He says, "No way." I look in the telephone book to find someone to teach me how to drive. I pay a driving school to teach me. I head off to the DMV, where I quickly pass my written test. While taking the driving part, I see a car coming to a red light. I feel that it isn't going to stop. I hesitate. It's a smart choice. The driver would have hit me. I pass the driving portion as well. Now that I have my license I will need my own car. I'm always good at saving. I have my money ready.

Charlie takes me to look for a car. I want to look around, but Charlie will only take me to the Honda dealer. I want to have an Outback style of car, but I have to take what I can get. I purchase a new 1993 Honda Accord. I'm so excited to be able to drive myself to any place I need to go. The steps to becoming a real person are falling into place.

Charlie and I have been together many years. It's time we talk about being married. The time comes, and Charlie and I marry in October. My sisters and a few close friends attend our Las Vegas wedding. I'm not going to waste money on a big wedding. I have big dreams for Charlie's and my future. I walk myself down the aisle.

In November 1993 I apply for a job at Children's Wonderland. I'm hired right away. Shortly after I start, the administrator shares a letter with me from a parent stating that she had been very frustrated with the quality of care her child had been receiving and that until I started, she had been ready to pull her child from the program. She likes my method of dealing with children and could see that I have a good rapport with them.

I start work and make changes in the children for the better; I have a lot of patience and can handle them on their level. I work with the two-year-olds. They are very active. I love it, as I have always been overactive. I love my job. I still need more child-development classes in order to get more money. Again my boss calls me into her office. I'm nervous, not knowing why I'm being called in. My boss shares an awesome letter, stating that I should continue my education to advance in the childcare field.

Although my car is new, it's giving me a great deal of trouble. The motor mounts go out. The brakes go and the transmission dies. I have learned from past experience with my family that insurance is important. I had taken out a 100,000 mile coverage plan on it, and never missed a servicing. Fighting with the Honda dealership is very difficult. I lose it and scream at them, "You find out what is wrong with this lemon." I will not take this car off the dealership's property until they fix it. The insurance company tries to get out of the deal, but I've never missed an oil change or servicing. It's all been done at this dealership. They tell me they will pull it apart, but if they find nothing wrong I will be billed. After driving this lemon, I know they will find a problem: They take it apart and find a cracked cam. I am given a rental car until it is fixed.

CHAPTER 20

I'm not feeling well. I have started going for medical attention at Urgent Care. I tell the doctor I have a sinus infection. It's blocking in my head, causing a lot of pain. I explain that I boil water to steam my sinuses. I show the doctor a hard glop that came out. It's causing a lot of pain in my head; it's very hard to breathe. He gives me some medication. I ask, "Can you please take a sinus MRI or CAT Scan?" He doesn't feel tests are needed. I'm sent home.

Major headaches start. I've never had headaches. I return to Urgent Care. The doctor says, "You've had brain surgery. The sinus infection is affecting the surgery area." But I know it isn't my surgery area. How come I have trouble breathing all of a sudden? I've never had any problems until now. Something isn't right. The doctor gives me medication for asthma.

I'm still working each day at Children's Wonderland, enjoying my work. The headaches hurt to the point where when I get off work, I sleep. The smell in the house doesn't help. I return to the doctor.

The doctor sets me up for an x-ray. I know that my brain x-rays, never tell the truth; they do not show seizures. This only gets me worked up—that I'm not having a sinus CAT Scan to get the problem fixed.

The x-ray comes back, and he tells me that nothing is wrong. I have HMO insurance, but I can't see a specialist unless the HMO doctor sends me. This doctor doesn't want the money to go into another doctor's pocket. I keep right on his toes. He chooses drugs over testing, but the drugs have side effects, causing urinary-tract problems time after time. My body doesn't react well with the drugs this doctor is pushing. The doctor doesn't believe I'm experiencing side effects. He's on the drug maker's side. I listen to my body and stop taking the drugs.

I quit my job to return to school. I'm back in school, but it's not long before I can't take living at this apartment any longer. I say, "Something isn't right." I start to go through the house. I learn that everything is destroyed by a broken pipe. It's a tragedy. I refer to my renter's insurance, only to learn that there's no coverage for a rotten pipe. What a mess.

I find another place to live. We have nothing to our names. The situation allows me to see life in a different way. Where does a person pick up as life moves on? We move into another place, with nothing.

I continue college as Charlie continues to work. I'm lucky that I still have my parrots. Otherwise, we have nothing in this new place. It's a difficult life-problem to handle. I purchase some new clothes and a foam bed. It's a challenge to start over. I listen to the song "Starting All Over Again," which is really helping me hold strong. I know that I'm not the only one in life with problems.

I'm doing great in college. In my classes, people have no idea that I'm having such problems. People come up to me, wishing to be me. I just smile and think, "They should be careful what they wish for in life." The teacher says that she wants to speak to me after class. I say, "What have I done?" I stay after class to find out what she wants, and she asks if I want to work in the two-year-old classroom. I say, "Yes." I'm hired to be at school plus work at the same time.

CHAPTER 21

I get a call from Charlie's work. He has been run over by a loader. The lady says, "He is at the hospital in Ventura." I drop everything to go check on Charlie. The loader has run over his legs. "How did it take place?" It's still an unanswered question. We are living in an upstairs apartment. I carry him up as best I can. We have just lost everything. It's a mess. I still continue school and work. I need money to eat and pay bills. I thank God that I have never used credit cards; I have only paid as I spent. I have my Discover card, just to have credit, but I've never used it.

I'm very sick. My stomach is upset. I take Charlie to the doctor. We go in together, and the doctor sees me first. I tell him my stomach is still sick. He starts joking about my weight. I'm only 135 pounds. Charlie jumps in. I say, "You want to see me fat, I will teach you fat." He has no idea what is wrong with me, saying "It's stress." I say, "It isn't stress. I'm very sick. There is a difference." We leave his office without medical care—only a bill.

I take Charlie to the doctor's office, work, and try to finish college. Again a terrible blow hits us. There are heavy rains, and the roof is starting to collapse. All of our belongings, which don't amount to much, will be destroyed. I can't take any chances. We have a six-month lease. I go to the office and have it cleared to get out. I hurry to put everything into storage.

I find another place to live, and take Charlie to the new house. I go to pick up our things from storage, and learn that someone stole everything. Someone took my rod iron cages, clothes, and everything else. I wonder "How much more can a person take?" I go to the insurance company and say, "I tried to save things, and still lost them." This time I'm given a little money to get some clothes to wear.

We are now in a new place. I have no interest in replacing anything. I purchase a very little refrigerator, just big enough to keep milk in. I buy clothes. My parrots have no cages. I have them in a carry cage, which they can't live in. I have to give my birds a home where they will get great care, except for Ernie. She's my favorite parrot. I give the other birds to someone I know. It isn't easy to part with them.

CHAPTER 22

I return to the doctor, still with major sinus problems. Also, my left side has a very sharp pain, like I'm being stabbed. I still feel like I have the flu without a fever all of the time. He comes into the room, shaking his head. He says, "You have nothing on your left side." I say, "I have something. It feels like I'm being stabbed. The pain hurts really badly." The doctor answers, "I have no idea what it could be." I say, "When I find out, I will make sure that you will be the first one to know what it is and what is done to fix it." I ask him, "What's this flu-type feeling?" He says, "You have a lot of stress." I say, "It isn't stress. It's what we call life. I'm having medical problems." He says, "You need to slow down." I tell the doctor, "I have no time to waste. I still have a lot to get done before April 10, 2006." I tell the doctor, "I'm fulfilling my dream." He just looks at me as if I'm full of hogwash.

I've been put on one drug after another. It's affecting my system, causing urinary problems. In all of my years, I never had urinary problems, until after taking all those drugs. I ask the doctor "Can't you set up a brain test and a sinus MRI or CAT Scan?" Again he doesn't feel tests are needed. I look at this man, asking, "Why don't you doctors take tests? Is it to save the insurance company money, or do you get bonuses as you're killing the patients?" He isn't very happy. I'm to a point where I don't care. I have terrible headaches with sinus problems, repeated urinary tract infections from the medications, plus these oddball side effects. My left side feels like I'm constantly being stabbed. I'm becoming more run down. I'm still attending college plus looking after Charlie.

Charlie isn't right. Something is wrong. I notice changes as I take Charlie to the doctor to get care.

The doctor says, "Charlie is fine." I say, "That's because you're not around him all day." He doesn't think anything is wrong. Nothing is going to be done, so I take Charlie back home.

The stress from one bad thing after another is taking its toll on me. My grades are slipping, and I'm having trouble concentrating. Again I find myself at the post office, changing our address for the third time in just a short period. I stand in line and ask God to not give me any more struggles. I'm falling apart. Charlie is released to go back to work, but the company places him in another field forty-five miles away. I take Charlie to work, go to classes, observe classes, then pick Charlie up. Charlie is becoming concerned with my driving, as I seem to zone out at times due to stress.

I drop out of college, and that cuts me out of my job since I'm required to attend classes to be able to work. I'd heard about a new daycare center— Kinko's Little K Kids—that opened while I was working at Children's Wonderland. I apply to work for this company. I'm hired to cover for a teacher who is having a baby. My life becomes busier. I drive Charlie to his work, do my job, run to the post office and other errands and go back to pick Charlie up. We have nothing except the clothes on our back.

The stress is too much for me. It's time to go pick up the mail from the post office, but I forget how to get there. I'm driving around and around. Finally I have to ask someone if they can tell me where the post office is located. They point and say that it's just around the corner. I go to there, but I can't remember my box number. I use my key on box after box, hoping someone doesn't notice me. I keep trying until my key opens the right one. I leave the post office to go home. I can't remember where I live. Nothing looks familiar. It takes me three hours to find my home. It's a scary moment for me.

I call Dr. Sam immediately after arriving home and set up an appointment for the next day. I write down my box number, along with my correct address, and put it in my wallet. I go to pick up Charlie from work. Charlie is showing changes, and I tell this to his doctor, asking if he can run a brain test on Charlie. But again he doesn't think that tests are needed.

I take Charlie to work and go to see Dr. Sam. I drop everything on his lap. He tells me I have post-traumatic stress disorder, a result of all the years of stress, and he prescribes Serzone to help me get through the hard times. I talk about my sickness, the pains that the doctors have blamed on stress and brain surgery. He listens as I unload years of hurt and rejection. I explain how I had been abused while growing up, and how the doctors' conclusion that my seizures were for attention caused me more grief at home. Dr. Sam tells me how sorry he is for all that happened. I ask him, "If I save the money will you please set up all the tests to get the correct medical treatment to let medical doctors see that my brain is fine?" He answers, "Yes." Emily, his nurse, is in the room listening to this entire conversation taking place. He never tells me The Epilepsy and Brain Mapping Program does not accept his cash patients to have brain test done. I leave my neurologist's office believing his word.

I continue working. The Serzone is doing great. I really like my job at Kinko's Little K Kids. Staff members love my work, calling me Mary Poppins. They wish that they had my energy and my cheerful, positive attitude.

One day I take Charlie to work and he quickly returns to the car telling me he has been told to go home and wait for a call. I tell him, "That's their nice way of saying you are fired." He becomes angry and says he isn't fired. We return home. I give our thirty-day notice to the apartment, telling the manager that we will be moving. I purchase a one-way ticket to Idaho. We have property there that is paid off, for my dream. I take Charlie to the doctor to get his medications, and I call his family to pick him up. I give him $2,000.00 dollars, taking him to the airport for him to head to Idaho.

CHAPTER 23

My brother Ron again enters my life. Of course there is a reason for his return. He needs money. I tell him I have no money; it's all being used to get medical attention. He asks if he can use my Discover card. Knowing his background, I'm afraid to help him. However, my kind heart remembers the times he helped me with rides to the hospital. Again I make a mistake. This time I draw up an agreement: should he fail to pay me back, I can sell his truck to pay off the credit card. I have borrowed the money on my credit card. I'm really worried about the outcome. First Ron Jr. is good; he's making payments when they are due. Sadly, the money he can afford to pay me hardly covers the interest, let alone the loan amount. I never see any more money come my way; I have to pay the bill to keep my credit clean.

I'm still working at Kinko's. One of the ladies I work with has a room for rent. This will really help me a great deal, as money is tight. I also approach my boss for a raise, but I'm turned down. None of my co-workers realize what I'm going through. There is an opening for a full-time teacher. I quickly apply. I'm again turned down and decide I have given all I have. I get the newspaper and apply for a live-in nanny job. I apply for several, but am not successful in getting hired. Things are getting worse; the room I rented is needed for the co-worker's son, who is returning home. I have until November 1, 1997 to get a new place to live *and* a new job. I'm hired for the next nanny job I apply for. I give my notice to Kinko's and my boss suddenly offers me the raise I have asked for. It's too late. My friend Betty will keep my favorite parrot Ernie until I can pay off my car and get back on my feet.

With all that's taking place I'm still trying to keep my head above water. I look over the newspaper to see what else is available; I'm going to need a second job for awhile as well. I find one; it's modeling. I say "How hard can modeling be to stand and smile? I'll give it a try." I call to make my appointment. I'm set up; they want me to bring nice clothes. It pays $175.00 an hour. It sounds great. I go for my appointment. "Your eyes," he says "are beautiful. You look like a winner." All I want is to have my car paid off and some extra money to go home to build my child care.

One hundred seventy-five dollars sounds like a lot. They are taking many pictures. He says, "I'd like to do some bathing suits, bras and underwear." I'm nervous on bras and underwear. I tell myself, "What's the difference from a bathing suit?" I go for it. He looks at my smile and says, "That's your new name, "Smiley." The pictures come out great. I have very large breasts. They ask, "Are you Dolly's sister?" I say no as I smile, take the check and leave.

Time goes by. The phone rings, and it's the company, calling me back, wanting me to come into the office to talk about more pictures. I go to the office. Paul starts to compliment my beautiful smile, and my great personality. He says, "You have very large breasts." He wants me to do nude pictures. "You have the body that will make you a millionaire." I say, "I'm sorry; I'm not interested in nude pictures." He continues, "You have the breasts to show it." I said to myself "That's all I need is to have nude pictures floating around showing off my large breasts to everybody; having parents notice it from the Internet or magazine, me, being a child care provider." "No thank you." I insist, "I'm not interested in nude pictures." He says, "How do you think these women make it big?" I answer, "I guess I will continue to be poor."

I'm thankful for the money I did make, to pay my bills. What was ever done with all the pictures, I have no idea. I just take this as a lesson that modeling isn't my kind of lifestyle. I will not take myself down that low. The world looks large, but it's too small to hide from cameras and the public.

CHAPTER 24

On November 1, 1997 I start the live-in nanny job. I take care of two little boys. This will keep my bills paid and I will send to Charlie in Idaho the boxes, containing the few belongings we have left. I make sure the boys are getting great care. We play games; we fly kites made of bags. Sadly, life is again to hurt me. The father of the boys starts to make passes at me. Living in their home becomes uncomfortable for me, so I rent a room from an elderly lady.

Betty calls; the lady who has been keeping my parrot says she is no longer able to take care of her. I have no place to keep her. My younger sister Patricia calls to tell me she will keep Ernie for me. I'm relieved, and give her the bird to care for until I can take my parrot to Idaho with me. This is a poor decision on my part, as my sister crosses me. It's not long before I receive a call from my niece, who wants four hundred dollars in order for me to buy Ernie back. She tells me her mother has sold Ernie to a pet shop. I have no extra money; I have lost Ernie forever. I ask, "Where was my parrot sold?" I'm told at a swap meet in La Mirada, California. It just kills me. Ernie was like a child to me.

I continue my nanny job until Presidents' Day 1998, a day I will not forget right away. I have the two little boys down for their nap. Their mom is at work, their dad is at home, but he is supposed to be out running errands. I'm cleaning the kitchen to have everything cleaned up before the children awaken. I hear a noise in the doorway. There stands the father with his pants down. He says, "Look what I have for you." I tell him I'm not interested. I turn from him and continue to do the dishes. He comes closer to me. I grab a butcher knife. He does not come any closer. I can smell the alcohol on his breath. He goes into the bedroom and passes out on the bed. I want badly to stab his eyes out with the butcher knife. The song "Bohemian Rhapsody" by the rock band Queen sings in my ears. I've already lived with abuse; the anger inside is exploding. His wife is working in the Navy. She is on her evaluations for her job; I don't want to interrupt her evaluations. I stay on my job until the wife is finished. I speak to a family friend, making sure he knows what took place. He's in shock, having a hard time believing me. I can't see leaving two children with a drunken man. I'm angry. I call a friend of mine. He says, "You should feel proud. It should let you know you're a beautiful woman." I only feel disgusted.

The children's mother is now finished with her evaluations. I sit her down and I share with the woman what has happened, and I resign from the job. I still have two car payments to make in order to be debt free. I return to Kinko's; luckily they have an opening so I'm not without work for long.

I get a letter from the father, saying how sorry he is for what he has done to me, and that it's not my fault. He would like to tell me he is attending AA meetings to get help. Again I just make sure that his children did not get left with a drunken man. I know my job is done; I've made sure two children have great care, plus made sure they are looked after.

CHAPTER 25

I return to my neurologist and tell him my most recent troubles. I tell him I will no longer take the Serzone, as its long-term effect is liver damage. I have again rented a room with a stranger. I'm desperate. The lady wants me to stay home and keep her company instead of working for a living. All of the bad things—the lack of repayment of the loan to my brother, the loss of my favorite bird, the attempted sexual assault by my employer—are too much for me. I give up and call Charlie, telling him I'm on my way home to Idaho. I leave at 11:00p. m., and drive twenty-six hours to get there. Upon arriving, I find all the doors locked. It's 1:00a.m. A neighbor, Dan, has his lights on, so I go to him for help. Charlie is on seizure medication that is too strong, and he is overdosed. He is passed out on the bed. I quietly climb into bed to sleep until 8:00 in the morning.

I call Charlie's doctor to talk with him about the medications they have prescribed for Charlie. He is passed out; obviously it is far too strong. I have to carry Charlie over my shoulder to the car to get him to the doctor. Had I waited any longer, he would have died from the effects of this medicine. At this point, I'm a pro at fighting with doctors, and stand my ground.

Over a four-day period, the doctor takes Charlie off all medicines. I know that if Charlie has no medicine the uncontrolled seizures will start again. I beg the neurologist to give me two milligrams of Lorazepam to put under his tongue, when needed. The doctor doesn't feel this drug is needed, but I know that if your body doesn't get the drug, after so long it will attack.

Sure enough, three days later, Charlie starts to have the uncontrolled seizures; one right after another. I'm on the phone to his doctor to call in the Lorazepam prescription. I leave Charlie to get the prescription. I come back crushing them; sticking them under his tongue until the seizures stop. The doctor tells me to take Charlie for a blood test. I have no faith in doctors or their treatment of people. I have been through so much and have to fight all the way. They say a doctor practices medicine; guess what, he practices on you!

We live in one house while I work on my dream. The house is very old, needing lots of fixing up, but I have a vision of what it can be. The man next door, Dan, is helpful to me from my first night there. Charlie is unable to help; Dan is always there, with the start of remodeling on the little house that will soon be Laura's Little House Child Care. New windows, paint, and hours of hard work; I put in everything I have to get it started, to run my own center. I wish my mother could see everything I have accomplished. I know my mother would be very proud.

CHAPTER 26

November isn't a good time to open a day care center in Idaho; many people are getting laid off or snowed in. I decide to open my doors anyway. The lack of children allows me to take Charlie back and forth to the doctor when needed. Little by little, children are enrolling in my little house. Every penny I make goes back into the house to make it a better place for the children. Charlie puts me down and says I have a stupid job. I try to share with him my dream of buying the two homes across the street also. He makes fun of me, saying I couldn't do that while watching other people's kids. He tells me it will never happen. My first group of kids are problem kids that nobody else wanted to care for. They are rude and wild. This is just what I wanted. I have a gift for out-of-control little people, and I work on their self-esteem to change their behaviors. To everyone's amazement, it works. The children seem to calm down and become better mannered. Of course I know what they need, as I myself have been that low-self-esteem child.

Charlie is not the man I married. The accident has really changed him. He has mood swings and becomes very angry for no reason. I have no idea what I should do. I'm not sure how violent he can become. I'm reading the Bible and hoping for an answer. Charlie takes my Bible and throws it in the mud, screaming at me to get out.

The state people come to look over the little house. It still needs lots of work. They tell me how I can get money to help replace the fence. I fill out all the papers and a check comes my way. I still have to wait until I have the rest of the money. Now I'm in compliance. The state workers are very impressed with what I've been doing with the children. And I'm so happy watching the children play, knowing nobody will abuse them or say mean things to them.

CHAPTER 27

It's time for me to see my neurologist in California. I don't want to start over with a new neurologist— I'm tired of starting over with new doctors. I purchase my ticket and arrange for Tonya to pick me up from the airport. I leave to see my doctors.

My neurologist is always in a hurry. I let him know I'm saving for my test, but that with everything else coming at me it will take time. I have major medical problems, and it's going to take a brain test to prove medical doctors wrong and to get the proper care. They still insist my current health problems are due to my brain surgery. He is glad to see that I'm hanging in there, as my appointment ends. I pay and leave.

I go see the doctor at Urgent Care, telling him I'm still having the same problems. He gives me samples of Vioxx. I take this drug, like he has told me to. By the third day I'm starting to have tightness in my chest and chest pains; my chest feel like someone's pulling it apart. I stop taking the drug right away. I call the doctor, and am told to go to his office. I go in to see him, telling him this drug is attacking my heart. I'm in a lot of pain; I've never had heart problems. He says Vioxx doesn't affect the heart. I say "Call me crazy, but if I continue taking this drug it will kill me." He says that my stress has me jumping to conclusions. I answer, "You remember this visit. I will come back when it's pulled off the market. Given my same feedback, you will see I'm not wrong." I play him the song "Blowin' in the Wind" as I leave his office.

Before I leave I tell myself, "Read what is written in your records." I return to his office, asking the lady in charge, "Would you please pull my records—I would like to look them over." She takes me into a back room. She watches me look over my records, reading what the doctor wrote. He writes that I have arthritis and anxiety from the years of life problems. I'm so angry I pull those papers out of my records. The lady tells me that I'm not allowed to remove them from my files. I say "You've seen nothing; this man is going to learn in time he gave me a killer drug. "You will see this drug will be pulled off the market because other people will complain of the same thing." I don't like lies in my records. I destroy the papers. I leave California, returning home.

CHAPTER 28

Across the street there is a lady in her eighties. I have been friendly with her and know that she raises her blinds at the same time every morning, taking walks to go have breakfast at five o'clock. The lady's son and his wife come once in a while to check on her.

One day I notice the blinds are not raised. I call the police and they contact her son Ray. Sure enough, the lady has taken a bad fall as a result of a stroke. She was rushed to the hospital to get checked out. Eventually, she is able to return home.

Ray approaches me about keeping an eye on her. I always call her grandma; she does not mind at all. Ray's mom loves to work in the yard; she sits on the ground with scissors and edges her yard. She leaves for a walk to the store. I tell Charlie to get the lawn mower, and we run over to her yard to cut her grass and make her grounds look nice. She returns, telling me her son must have come. I just smile. It makes me feel good, and it's good for Charlie to be nice to someone. Ray comes to see his mom. I tell him how Charlie and I snuck over and mowed her lawn. We are watching her carefully. Ray's wife is telling Ray that I really like him. I don't even know the man— only as the elderly lady's son. Again someone thinks that I wanted more than friendship. This makes me angry. My sole purpose is to help the little old lady who lives across the street. Sadly, the lady continues to have strokes and falls. Unable to stay alone, she moves into a nursing home. Ray says he will soon be selling her house.

My daycare center is doing okay. I'm saving money to buy the children educational toys and a giant wagon so I can pull them around. Finally I save the money and am able to order our wagon. I put a sign on the front of the wagon reading "Who Supports Our Children?" This gets local businesses rallying together to support the children by offering their contributions. The children and I sit down, making thank-you cards for all who supported us.

Charlie continues to treat me badly. I decide I have to get out. I approach Ray and ask if I might buy his mom's house. I do not want to give up my daycare. My bond with the children is very strong.

I'm still very sick. It feels like the flu, with bad headaches and a really sharp pain in my left side, like I'm being stabbed. August of 2000 I will try my luck once again with doctors, only because the pain is so bad. I'm told Mountain Health Care is a good place. I go see the doctor, filling out the papers, making sure it's all correct, to get medical attention.

I'm again told my pain is a result of brain surgery. The doctor starts in on my weight. I say, "A doctor used this already when I was at 135 pounds." He argues back that brain surgery can affect people in different areas. I demand that a brain test be done, to prove the doctors wrong. I'm not going to give up.

I again ask Ray about buying his mom's house. He tells me to go for it. I hurry to the bank and apply for a loan. Interest rates are very high, but I say I will do some changing later. Charlie is getting worse. He calls me bad names and tells me to get out. I smile and leave; I buy the house across the street, and then file for a divorce. The house that Charlie and I lived in and the house I used for my daycare remained in both of our names. Charlie continues to live in the house we shared, and I continue running my daycare in the other one. I've gone from having no home to owning two homes, and running my own daycare center. If only my dad were alive to see it.

Ray comes by to see me, showing me a note he has found under the mattress that his wife has written to his friend. The note talks about their time together, when Ray had thought she was with a female friend. He's totally crushed, needing me to help him get through it. Now I understand why she said that I was trying to make a pass at Ray; she was looking for a way out of her marriage. I support him through the divorce process, as I have recently gone through it and know what to expect.

Ray continues to work in the mines and to care for the two stepsons his ex-wife has left behind. Like me, he cannot turn his back on children in need. The boys are in high school. I'm making sure I help them with school projects; it becomes a team effort to finish the job of raising the boys. After a period of time, the boys decide to go to live with their grandmother. Ray and I support them in their wishes.

CHAPTER 29

I'm still having bad headaches, and I'm afraid my seizures will come back if I don't get treatment for my sinus troubles. It's July 9, 2001. I have worked hard to save the money to update all of my brain tests, so I fly to California to see Dr. Sam again.

My office visit is interrupted by staff members. He steps out, returns, and says "Okay, Lori, I will see you in a year." Out of the room he goes; I think nothing of it. I pay for my visit, and leave his office to update my brain test.

I call Alex and ask, "Do you have openings for a Brain MRI, CAT Scan and EEG test?" He says, "Yes." "I will need Dr. Sam's orders." I don't feel it will be a problem. I call his office. Of course, speaking to a doctor directly is next to impossible. His staff wants to know what insurance I will be using. I state, "I have none, but I saved the cash for my brain test." They of course do not think I will have enough money. They ask me "Where is your money coming from? Do you know how much these tests cost? I answer, "Yes." I don't feel it's the woman's business where the money is coming from. I ask, "Can you please have Dr. Sam return my call as soon as possible?"

After days of playing phone tag, I'm told that The Epilepsy and Brain Mapping Program doesn't accept Dr. Sam's cash patients. I'm told to find a place that accepts cash. I check with local facilities that offer such testing. Both UCLA and Long Beach Memorial accept cash and can do my brain test as long as Dr. Sam gives them the orders.

I call, asking to speak to Dr. Sam; my brain tests are all blocked. It's time to leave California. Now I'm angry that I have spent money on a plane ticket, unable to get the testing done that I needed. I trusted my neurologist.

I do not drop the ball there. I contact The Epilepsy and Brain Mapping Programs office again, asking to speak to the office manager and explaining the entire process one more time. I explain how I have flown in and am unable to get my brain test updated because I'm paying by cash and have no insurance. The lady in charge listens, saying she will look into it and will get back to me. Dr. Sam had never warned me that his facility doesn't accept his cash patients.

The woman calls me back, ready to schedule my MRI at a place close to my home. I tell her I want a plane ticket to return to California to have these tests done at my neurologist's facility. They are unable to provide the ticket, but do find Kootenai Medical Center in Coeur D'Alene Idaho to do my MRI on July 25, 2001.

The MRI results are in, confirming what I've been saying all along: my brain is perfectly fine now. I'm ready to get medical attention. My MRI will give it a start. I will still need an EEG and a CAT Scan to prove to the doctors that without a doubt, my brain is fine.

I schedule an appointment with an ear, nose and throat specialist. I tell the doctor that my sinuses have been blocked since 1994, and here we are in 2001. The infection is in my head and I'm in a lot of pain. I explain that I have terrible headaches and I feel as though I have the flu all the time. I experience odd feelings; sometimes I feel very dizzy and the walls appear to be moving. Then it all changes suddenly, my head feels as if it's being hit with a hammer, my left eye feels like someone is trying to poke it out, and my left arm loses circulation; like someone has tied a tourniquet around it. I have stabbing pains in my left side just below my rib cage. He starts to say, "You've had brain surgery." I immediately stop him and show him my MRI; my brain is fine. He promises to schedule me for a CAT Scan of my sinuses.

I call time after time, leaving messages for my neurologist to call me as soon as possible. I wait and wait, still fighting to get medical attention to cover all of my sickness and pain. The rest of my brain test needs to be done. Nothing comes my way. July, August, September, and October 2001 pass, but still nothing. I will have to write a letter to see if that will work. Irritated, I mail a letter to Dr. Sam, asking him to call me as soon as possible.

November 13, 2001 comes. Four months have passed, and finally Dr. Sam calls. I say, "My tests are not being called in for someone to do." He's really sorry. I ask him, "Who made the rule that your cash patients can't be tested at The Epilepsy and Brain Mapping Program?" He cannot answer. I say, "You can find out from your nurse. Then let me know." I continue, "Why didn't you warn me that cash patients can't be tested at The Epilepsy and Brain Mapping Program?" You've left me a victim: Alex had the time to do all of my brain tests plus I have the cash to pay for them. All Alex needed was for you to okay it, but that never took place." He explains, "They are trying to get you help." I say, "All the help I need is for you to give someone the okay for all of my brain tests to be updated." He shares that he couldn't set up any test. I will have to find someone who accepts cash and will do the rest of my brain test. Patients just can't set up a test; that has to be done by medical doctors. He shares, "Some patients who pay by cash do get brain tests done." I say, "Except mine." Dr Sam asks me, "Can I help with anything else?" I say, "I need to have my brain test completed. The

Epilepsy and Brain Mapping Program doesn't accept my cash, and you won't give anybody else the okay for my brain test to be done. No; but please clear my name with your staff members. You told me that if I saved the money you would set up all the brain tests at your facility. You lied to me, and I believed your words. I'm a patient who has the cash to pay for all of my brain tests. You will see, in time I will find a way." We concluded our conversation.

Dr. Bob starts working in the valley, so I go to see him. I say, "I have a very sharp pain in my left side. I feel like I have the flu, without fever. I have these off-the-wall side effects. One day I'm very dizzy, and the walls appear to be moving. My head hurts like I just had brain surgery—you can't touch it. And I'm very tired and weak. Then it changes. My head feels like its being hit with a hammer. I can feel my heart beat in my stomach and feet. My left eye feels like someone's trying to poke it out and my whole body is in a lot of pain, then if I'm active, I have trouble breathing. I dump everything on this doctor. I say "If you don't stop this left-side pain, I will take a gun and shoot two bullets into my left side, and make you doctors have to dig to find it." He says, "I will try my best." He sets me up with a blood test.

CHAPTER 30

I never would have dreamed that Ray and I would marry. We ask if the preacher could marry us in our car, but he doesn't perform weddings in cars. So we trudge through the snow and are married in a small church in Kellogg, Idaho in December, 2001. The wedding is attended by a friend, Willa, and her son and his wife. After the wedding we go to eat dinner. Willa says she had never seen a wedding like this one. I move in with Ray, and have someone rent my house.

I return to see Dr. Bob. The test came back, showing that I have costochondritis. I have no idea what costochondritis is. At this point, I don't care; all I want is the pain to be gone. Dr. Bob puts me on medication. In a couple of days the pain is gone. I ask Dr. Bob, "Does brain surgery cause costochondritis?" He laughs, saying no, knowing what is written in my medical files. Later, I find out that costochondritis is inflammation of the cartilage that joins the ribs to the breastbone; this is what has been causing my severe chest pain.

The ear, nose and throat specialist calls, saying he wants to see me again. The tests have come back, showing that an infection has spread into my head. I'm not surprised. He tells me that I need medication. I explain that my neurologist's nurse Emily has been keeping my Biaxin prescription filled because the doctors don't treat me. He tells me he has to do surgery to open my sinuses, and he lets me see the blockage. I don't care what takes place. I just want the pain to be gone. He schedules me for sinus surgery for June 20, 2002.

I'm still running my own childcare center. Children have been like medicine for me, keeping me strong and with a reason not to give up. And music has always played its part, singing into my ears.

I close down the childcare to get ready to fight against medical doctors. I don't care what it takes. I'm ready to fight strong and hard.

June 20, 2002 is here. I go to the Kootenai Medical Center to have my sinus surgery. The gas mask causes me to remember the major brain surgery. I smile and say, good luck.

I come out of the operation just fine. I follow the doctor's rules following the surgery, and then return to his office. Everything has come out great—no more sinus problems. I ask the doctor if the trouble was caused by brain surgery, and he tells me no.

Next I turn to the childcare center, to remodel it like I first wanted to. I take it down to its 2 x 4s, remodeling it from top to bottom. New plumbing, electric, walls, and flooring are installed. The medical bills take the money I had saved up to do the enlargement—which would have added on a den, bathroom and bedroom. So I just work with what I have. This is where my knowledge comes into play— everything I had learned at Fred's house. I believe he still looks over me to see that I'm doing my best.

Now that the daycare is closed, I have time to see the doctors. I also have the opportunity to look over my own records and read what is written. The last doctor has written some really bad things about me. He states that when I was trying to stop the sharp pain in my left side and the pain in my hip, I had jumped off of the bed and dropped my pants. Reading this makes me angry. Another doctor thinks I need psychiatric help. I say, "Wouldn't you if you'd been in my shoes, being mistreated by the medical community?" I just hope this mess will be found out soon, so I can let the doctors see I wasn't wrong and crazy.

CHAPTER 31

Time passes. Ray wants to retire from the mining company. I tell him, "Do what you want to do." He puts in his notice for retirement. He says, "It's a great feeling." He wants to see life. For me, who had been living in doctors' offices, I can understand. What do miners really see in life underground?

Ray is now retired and I'm still working on the little house. Ray says that he has never seen a woman do this kind of work. I say "It will look great once it's done." I'm off work. I tell Ray I will take him to my family's house. Tonya calls, asking if I want my mother's albums. I say "Yes, save them for me until I can get down there." Ray has no idea what I'm talking about. I tell Ray that I asked my father if I could have my mother's albums after she died; he's giving everything away before he dies. My father said the albums went to Tonya." But my mother and I were the ones who most enjoyed music; this is why Tonya is giving me our mother's albums.

Summer arrives and I say, "Let's go on a vacation. I've not been anywhere except work." We both take off. It sure is a great feeling to get out and do something besides work and fight with doctors. We arrive at Tonya's house. She isn't home so we go on to Jennifer's. I take Ray to show him the beaches, and Knox Berry Farm. I let him see where I grew up. Tonya's husband takes Ray to a baseball game. Ray is having the time of his life.

He says that traffic isn't bad. I take him to Oxnard, California to let him see many places. I stop to see the doctor I had known, plus see the places I'd worked at in the past years.

It's time to come home to my sister's house. I hit the 101 freeway at 4:30 in the afternoon to drive to

Long Beach. Traffic is all backed up from 101 to the 405 freeway; it's a mess. The cars don't move, so we don't arrive until 6:30. Ray learns about busy traffic. I enjoy letting Ray see something beside the mines. Tonya gives me our mother's records. I load them into the car and it's time to go home. It is a time Ray will never forget. We both enjoyed our time away.

We arrive at home. I get back to work on the little house. Ray has to always come to visit me while I work. The renters living in my house give me notice that they are moving out. Ray and I are still living in Ray's house in Kellogg. I say to Ray, "It will sure be easier if we just sold this house and moved into my house." Ray doesn't want to sell his house. I try persuasion, "Let's move into my house. I won't have to drive to work, plus you will be right here by me." He has to think about it. I let him think while I continue to do my work.

CHAPTER 32

My renters move out and I have to clean up. I don't want to be a landlord any more. I keep the house empty, fixing it up along with my little house. Ray comes to see me. I say, "If you live here you can be here all the time." Sure enough, it works. Ray says, "I will rent out my house." I tell him, "Renting isn't easy and it's work." Ray has worked only in a mine, having no idea about real life. He looks into the renter's field; he has a family he knows very well (he thinks) move into his house.

Ray and I move into the house across the street from the little house. It's great to be right here, not having to drive any more. I still have not purchased any furniture. I just live with what I have as life moves on. I have tried to go to stores to buy furniture, but end up telling myself I have lived this long with nothing. Why not longer? I'm looking to finish my journey in life, to have my goal accomplished by April, 2006.

The family is renting Ray's house. Ray is learning how people really treat you when doing business. We all have to learn by lessons. I was lucky at my house—I had great renters. Ray lets himself think all people are like this, but it isn't true. Ray says, "Let's sell the house." I say, "Go for it." I go to the real estate lady, whom I've always done business with, to put this house up for sale. I give the renters a month's notice, to give them time to move out. Once they move out I make sure the house is fixed up, to be sold as soon as possible. I'm glad to get out of the renting field. Ray asks me, "Why didn't you make me listen to you?" I say, "You needed to learn for yourself." Living in this house Ray sits and tries to understand, "How did I live in my house for so many years?" I say, "You've worked in the mines, raised your children, plus your three stepchildren. Now you've retired to see life."

CHAPTER 33

I'm still feeling very sick. I've had it with doctors. I call my sister Jennifer and tell her what is wrong. She tells me to stop using all dairy products for one month. I do this and the symptoms disappear. Jennifer tells me it's called lactose intolerance. I'm beginning to believe in more natural things and trying allergy tests rather than drugs. I begin to watch my own body and the symptoms that are occurring, documenting them. I start to put together all that the doctors have said. One reported that I have low blood pressure while another one said I have high blood pressure.

I start to write down my symptoms. One day I'm very tired and weak. My head feels like I had brain surgery the day before. It takes everything I have to keep going (low blood pressure).

Then it changes. My head is in pain; as if it's being hit with a hammer each time my heart beats. Then it feels like someone is pushing out my left eye. I can feel my heart beat in my feet and stomach. I have major pain in my left arm, like someone is tying a rubber band around it. My body is in a lot of pain-high blood pressure.

I return to Dr. Bob, telling him it's my blood pressure. I say, "I can show you. It jumps from extra low to high, then drops down again." He tells me to come in three times a week and we will check it twice a day. I say, "That will be great." It isn't. It causes more problems with the staff members at Mountain Health Care.

I come into his office. I stop at the front desk, saying that I'm here for my blood pressure. I'm told to be seated. My name is called. The nurse asks me, "Why are you here?" I repeat, "For my blood pressure."

The nurse takes my pressure, and it is low. I return in the late afternoon; it's still low. I leave, returning two days later, again saying I'm here for my blood pressure. The nurse calls me in saying that I don't need my blood pressure checked this often. I again tell her that I'm having blood pressure changes and that the doctor needs to see it. Now it's not reading right. I have to deal with nurses not wanting to do my blood pressure. I still keep returning, as I'm told to by the doctor, not caring how the nurses feel. I feel, why work at a medical building if you don't want to give medical attention? The staff becomes ugly with me, as the blood pressure checks show it's unbalanced.

I return to see Dr. Bob, saying, "Your staff told me I didn't need my blood pressure checked this much, but you can still see it jumping up and down. I know if it gets too low I just have to come here saying I'm here for a blood pressure test. I have to fight with your staff, and it makes it jump up for no reason. You have bad communication with your staff, telling me to come in for blood pressure tests. Then your staff tells me I don't need my blood pressure checked. It's best you tell your staff to get off of my back. Let me do what needs to be done. You can see it didn't stop me to show you it's my blood pressure." He puts me on medication.

Dr. Bob tells me to go see Dr. Horse, a neurologist in Coeur D'Alene, Idaho. I ask Dr. Bob, "Will you please set up all of my brain tests?" Again he doesn't feel that tests are needed.

I go to the neurologist on October 9, 2003. My name is called. I tell this neurologist everything again. As with all the doctors, he feels that it's caused by brain surgery. He says, "People don't feel their blood pressure. I say, "I feel it." I have never been like normal people and it looks like I will never be like normal people. Dr Horse thinks my headaches are caused by brain surgery. I say, "That's how much common sense you have in the neurology field." I ask this man, "How long have you been in the neurology field?" He answers, "About twelve years." I say, "That answers it; you're only a baby neurologist." I ask, "Can you please set up my CAT Scan, my EEG, plus my spine and neck MRI?" He doesn't feel that tests are needed. He thinks my headaches are caused by my 1986 brain surgery. Dr. Horse gives me a drug sample called Relpax. I take one sample at his office and take the other two at home. I leave his office without a brain test.

I have Ray fill the prescription at the drug store. It cost two hundred dollars for twelve pills; I come unglued. That money could have gone toward my brain test. Taking the Relpax drug samples doesn't do anything for my headaches. I call Dr. Horse, asking "How many days does it takes for it to work?". He tells me I have to just continue taking the drug. I answer, "Taking three pills costing almost twenty dollars each—who are you trying to make rich?" I go back to see Dr. Bob.

I'm at Dr. Bob's office. I say, "What kind of kook did you send me to?" I want to see Dr. Dice; he is a neurosurgeon. Dr. Bob tries to calm me down. I say, "You take two hundred dollars out of your pocket to get a drug that hasn't stopped uncontrolled headaches yet. That amount could have gone toward my EEG, my spine and neck MRI and CAT Scan." Dr. Bob says, "I can set up your brain MRI." I say, "I've already asked you how many times?" He answers, "I will set up the brain MRI." I tell him, "I've already had my brain MRI. I need my spine and neck MRI and my CAT Scan and EEG." He sets up another brain and Spine MRI, and still sends me to see a neurosurgeon.

I go to see the neurosurgeon. He looks over all of my medical records, plus the reason I'm in his office. "You're not the only patient who has been treated like this." I say, "All these doctors in Idaho have had bad education. It's sad that a part-brainless patient has more knowledge than them. UCLA should feel very proud that their brainless patient has more common sense than some doctors have."

The Neurosurgeon sets up any test that I say I need done. I ask, "Do you know a neurologist in our area who is on our level?" He says yes. Dr Smarts was once here in Coeur D'Alene, then left for Spokane, Washington." I say "Do you blame him for leaving if he's on our level?" Dr Dice just smiles, and makes no comment. He sets me up to go see Dr Smarts in Spokane and my brain and spine MRI results come back. My spine MRI shows arthritis in the spine and neck, and where I was hit by the car when I was two years old. The spine isn't right. It shows major spine damage. But my brain MRI has come out great. This helps me understand why I can't sit or be in one spot for very long. Knowing what is wrong makes it easier to deal with the pain. Not knowing what is wrong is what causes problems.

I go see Dr. Smarts on Feb 6, 2004. He looks over my records. Right away I say, "Don't believe what you are reading in those records. It's all lies." I ask, "How educated are you in this field?" He answers "Many years." I say, "You were smart not staying at the office in Coeur D'Alene. Those neurologists should have brain surgery themselves." The doctor makes no comment. I ask, "Have you heard about The Epilepsy and Brain Mapping Program?" He answers yes, I say, "Did you know they don't accept cash patients for brain tests?" He answers, no, and I say, "That's why I'm in your office." This doctor can tell I'm very angry. He takes the time to explain the body shakes, calling them tremors. I'm able to understand tremors from my childhood at UCLA. I say, "I remember tremors. I've always thought they were very small seizures." He explains, "They are nerves that shake different parts of the human body: legs, hands, and like yours, it shakes inside your body." He says he can put me on medication, and that it isn't anything to worry about. I ask Dr. Smarts if tremors are caused by brain surgery. He says no, understanding my anger. I know it wasn't from brain surgery, remembering it as a child at UCLA. I leave his office, thanking him for helping me understand why my body shakes all the time.

I return to Dr. Dice, with Dr. Smarts report. Dr. Smart wrote the truth. He doesn't want me back in his office. I have strong anger built up. He has other patients to handle, not wanting somebody else's mistreated patient. I tell Dr. Dice I'm glad he wrote the truth. I don't blame this doctor for not wanting to take over a patient who's been abused for eleven years. Dr. Dice says, "That's okay. We now know what the body shakes are caused by." I thank Dr. Dice for setting up the rest of my brain test. Now I will take it from here to fix these unknown medical problems. Dr. Dice says, "If you need anything else, just let me know." I leave his office.

It's really sad for anyone to have to fight this way to get tests done. Tests to doctors must be like poison; they don't like to give their patients tests.

The time has come. Vioxx is pulled off the market, following reports the same as my feedback from 1999. It's a drug that attacks the heart. I call the doctor making sure I talk to him on the phone.

He says I'm a very wise woman. I say, "Now the feedback is in; this drug does attack the heart." I ask the doctor, "Why didn't you believe me?" He says, "Doctors have to go by what drug makers report. It never said that it attacks the heart." I ask, "Now do you believe me?" He answers, "Many patients took the medication without having any effects. I believe it will come back on the market." I say, "If it does come back on the market they're going to read my 1999 report on it. It's a drug that attacks the heart." This doctor does not admit that he is wrong.

I find a cardiologist and call to have a heart test set up. I ask the lady, "Do these doctors know what they are doing?" The lady says, "They are great doctors. I would trust them." I'm scheduled to have my heart tested. I never had heart problems before I took that medication.

The test takes place, and the results indicate that I have breast implants. I have no idea where these implants have come from; I can't even tell you where I had them done. I call the office asking if I could speak to the doctor. I'm asked, "What is it you need?" I say, "My test came back, but the doctors can't read it correctly because of my breast implants. I had no idea I had implants!" She says that she will get back with me. I say, "Can you please have my money returned? I need to find a doctor who knows what he is doing. This doctor is a quack."

I call all the doctors I have seen in all the years, asking them if they put implants into my breasts. They all say no. I don't know how or when this happened.

CHAPTER 34

The work is now done. Laura's Little House is reopened, ready to let children learn while they can play and have fun in a safe environment. Parents are glad to see me return. The children are glad to be back to enjoy growing up.

The Real Estate lady calls, letting Ray and me know that she has found a buyer for the Kellogg house. She would like to set up a time to sign papers. She comes to our house. We sign papers, and the Kellogg house is sold. We both are so glad to get out of the rental field.

I have all of my brain tests done. I start to repeat tests that I can remember from UCLA. My phases were done for patients having headaches. At that time I had no headaches; mine were for seizures. I start to learn about foods. I purchase books on health and a healthy diet. I try eliminating particular foods to see if it makes a difference. Sure enough, my headaches stop as long as I stay away from foods with certain ingredients. Today I'm headache free. Headaches came from unbalanced blood pressure and certain ingredients in foods. I am now headache free.

The house next to ours is empty. I call the owner and ask if I can purchase the house. He comes to see the property. I don't care about the condition that it's in; I just want it to enlarge my yard. He wants out of the rental field and sells me the house. I tell the man, "Thank You:—you will see that it will put many smiles on children's faces." I go right to work to remove the old house. It's a lot of work to take it down. It has a full basement. I find a man with a tractor to remove the cement walls, and then I put gravel into the hole with four feet of good top soil.

I plant grass. Today it's a great yard to let children play and enjoy their development.

I work at the daycare and Ray enjoys the retired life. I say, "I've always wanted to go to Nashville. Music has always been my best friend, teacher and great medicine. It lets me know that I'm not the only one with hard times." When hard times come, a song sings into my ears telling me never to give up.

Today I start to take the children on a wagon ride. The man next door says, "Hi Mrs. Lori." I smile saying "Hello." The man says, "How would you like to buy this house?" My eyes open and see a large farmyard for the children. I ask how much, and he gives me a price. I say, "I will go to the bank to get a loan." I really still have the money in the bank from selling the Kellogg house. I go to get the money to purchase the property next to the little house. Now I have all the land I wanted to run my own childcare. I thank God every day for looking after the children and me.

I still want to go to Nashville, and start to look into it. I still have my 1993 Honda, and I spot a nice 2005 Caravan. I approach Ray about buying it. He says, "That's fine as long as it's not another house!" I wheel and deal with a local car dealership. I have the van delivered to my home and have my old car picked up. I pack my van and off Ray, Willa and I go to Nashville, the home of music. We stop in Branson, Missouri and see Mickey Gilley. Once it's over I say to Ray and Willa "I want to go talk to him." Willa and Ray stay seated. I go up to say "Thank you for all the years you sang into my ears. Music has been by my side from start to finish; it's been the best kind of medicine to keep me strong." Many times it's only fitting that when I plan a trip it is to a music city. We leave Branson for Nashville.

We are in Nashville, ready to take the bus tour to see the city. The driver says, "Dolly's sister is on our bus today." I know who he is joking about. While he's driving he says, "Look toward your right hand side. That's where Dolly gets all her clothes made. " I say, "Please stop! That's where I want to go." The tour is over. He shakes my hand and says, "Thank you for being a good sport." The trip is great. We see many country-western artists.

On the way home we stop in California to make sure I go to Urgent Care. I sign my name. I have to fill out papers for "Why are you here today?" I write to refill my Vioxx prescription and have my breast implants checked. My name is called to go into the room. The doctor is shocked to see me today. He came to the door looking over my files, and is busting up laughing. He comes in shaking his head. I hand him the papers that read that I have breast implants. He says that I should feel very proud for all I have been through in the years, and to be where I'm at in life today. I say, "You're reading more lies on that paper. I do not have breast implants. I find it insulting." He says, "For your age and your size most people have saggy breasts.

I say, "Let's take ourselves back to the start, when you said I was obese at 135 pounds. Notice my weight today. I'm going to make sure you see how big I can really get before my name is called. I tell you, I will teach you fat." He says, "You won't ever let me down on that one. I was only joking." Again, I don't take that as a joke. I let this doctor see that dreams do come true. He asks if I have stopped to see my neurologist. I say, "No, I was kicked out and all my brain tests were blocked because I was a cash-paying patient." He says, "You should still make sure he hears, 'I did it.'" He tells me I should be very proud, and again that I'm a very wise woman. I pay for my visit and leave his office.

We return from our trip. I have another piece of good news. I have been nominated for the NIAEYC award. This is an award given to outstanding daycare centers. I go to the dinner and win the award. The award is for working with children with disabilities. I have been the child, and now am the helping hand for the same type of children.

Where would I be today if I had not continued to fight for the correct medical attention? Again, nothing I had wrong with me had to do with my brain surgery. You can see I never let anything destroy my journey in life to have my dreams fulfilled.

I was the little girl who was the black sheep of the family who now owns my own home and daycare center. Would my daddy be proud of me today? I would be playing the Song "Do I Make You Proud?" to my daddy if he were still alive today.

I did it—I opened my own daycare center. I provide love and security to children, the love and security I had not received. My hard work and life experiences helped me become an awesome adult. Many children will grow strong as a result of the love and self-confidence I provide them with.

Dreams do come true.

We'd love to have you download our catalog of titles we publish at:

www.TEACHServices.com

or write or email us your thoughts, reactions, or criticism about this or any other book we publish at:

TEACH Services, Inc.
254 Donovan Road
Brushton, NY 12916

info@TEACHServices.com

or you may call us at:

518/358-3494